D1616831

BE YOUR OWN MESSIAH

Since 1966, I've responded to those who call me Fabio Novembre

5

Since 1992, I've responded to those who also call me 'architect'

I cut out spaces
in the vacuum
by blowing
air bubbles,
and I make gifts
of sharpened pins
so as to ensure
I never put on airs

My lungs are
imbued with
the scent of places
that I've breathed,
and when I
hyperventilate
it's only so I can
remain in apnoea
for awhile

As though
were pollen,
I let myself go
with the wind,
convinced...
able to seduce
everything that
surrounds me

I want
to breathe
till
I choke

I want
to love
till
I die

I Believe

I believe in architecture as a medium of communication. Perhaps it is less

modern than other contemporary media, but thanks to a three-dimensional

focus, it still displays an essential difference. Communication with human

bodies couldn't find a more appropriate vehicle within a reality expressed

primarily in images. Paradoxically, the relationship between light and

architecture, experienced by the most abused of our five senses, accentuates

the sense of contemplative enjoyment and shoves architecture back into a

two-dimensional aesthetic: a sphere of facile consumption.

[FN]

Fabio's inspiration? The most obvious source is the female body. Soft and supple curves flow through all his designs, and he doesn't deny their origin

Builder of Poems

[Leo Gullbring]

A wintry evening in Stockholm offered the delectable promise of John Caird's staging of A Midsummer Night's Dream. The reviews were excellent, and friends were raving about the production. I arrived at the theatre with such high hopes. Admittedly, the set design was enchanting and the cast terrific, especially the actor who played Puck. But what a linear adaptation. What an obedient queue of sights and sounds, all fearful of losing their places. Where was the total experience that has come to represent our expectation of a Shakespeare play?

My mind drifted back in time to a theatre in Perugia and another version of the same play, presented by the Lindsey Kemp Company. I remembered a fairytale scene created by a forest of naked bodies, dark trees and lush foliage. The stage had taken on a life of its own as the audience watched a simultaneous potpourri of events bathed in ominous moonlight. We marvelled at twists and turns that led to strange romantic relationships nowhere to be found in the original script. We laughed as the actors took their bows and left the

theatre with us, continuing their performance on the street, relaxing in a local bar, matching us drink for drink.

Discovering Fabio Novembre's work was bound to evoke a memory of the vast difference between those two

performances. While so many designers cling desperately to the obvious, Fabio's poetic approach is marked

by the search for a total experience of the type associated with the theatre. He invites you to enter an

imaginary landscape, a place that offers a palette of sensory teasers rather than a single narrative. Here lurks a

whole collection of stories waiting to be discovered.

Novembre exemplifies a number of Italian designers who adhere to the 'Shakespearean' quest for a total art.

They want their work to entangle the senses, to lead the mind into an imaginary mire, to create a present so

overwhelmingly immediate that it's able to overturn and reconfigure both past and future. Their goal is to make

opera d'arte, to invest form and matter with magic, to give their work a life of its own, to design objects that

transcend the need for interpretation. These men and women want art, design and architecture to question

what life is all about and to challenge our concepts of reality and virtuality – not to fall victim to the deadening

blows of a consumer society. This idealistic vision is in need of defenders – people willing to reject the

prevailing flash and desolation of minimalism, to turn their backs on postmodern irony and to ignore obscure

upstarts like cognitive ergonomics.

One vehement defender voices his protest all the way from Lecce in the southeast Italian region of Puglia.

Fabio Novembre possesses that unpredictable streak of capriciousness that motivates the world of Italian

design to surprise us with one fuori serie after another. Fabio's fiercely individual flair and his aura of self-

assurance is, of course, no exception in Italy, where designers don't have to battle old styles and

contemporary trends in the manner of their counterparts in other Western countries. An Italian designer's very

existence is based on challenging the design icons that virtually litter the streets of Milan. The capacity of

Italian design to surprise has ancient historical roots: roots that go deeper than an Italian's inborn

understanding of beauty and form. Although the Renaissance – said to have begun in Italy in the 14th century

– was a direct ancestor of 'modernity', the concept of modernism completely failed to capture the hearts and

minds of Italians. While other countries adopted the style and its underlying theory as a natural consequence

of political revolution, Italy was left with an adolescent version of modernism, which refused to mature. Italian

futurists, metaphysicians and rationalists questioned and quarrelled with its promising but frightening aspects,

as did the followers of Arte Povera, Alchimia and Memphis. The deep crisis ultimately experienced by modernism occurred in Italy earlier than it did in many other countries – consider Antonioni's La Notte – and

designers reacted to the situation by moving into unexplored territory, with amazing results. Elsewhere the

modernist movement tried to reconcile industrial production with culture, but in Italy the two continued to have

separate though not contradictory identities. They were not destined for wedded bliss. The culture of crisis

born in the post-war era (following World War II) produced a wealth of Italian design and fashion: objects and

clothing successfully exported to all corners of the world. Not all the names are billboard icons like those that

send American society into a twitter, but every Italian can patriotically claim the pizza – as diametrically

opposed to a bland McDonald's burger and its gratingly bright surroundings as you can get – as an example

of Italian ingenuity: dynamic, adaptable and available in every combination imaginable.

There's an 'I don't care' attitude about Novembre's work that fails to disguise a very caring guy. Preoccupied

with the sensory qualities of his creations, he doesn't give a damn about what other designers think. He's

oblivious to styles, movements and manifestos. Fabio ploughs his own field, ignoring trends and often

approaching his task with a childlike ingenuousness. The result is an oeuvre admired by countless lovers of

design the world over. I'm certainly not the only one who appreciates his straightforward naivety, his vivacious

colours, his predilection for tactility and his abhorrence of all that is perfect and ordered. A typical Novembre

design is the Atlantique in Milan, a disco with flowers as chairs, a glittering shower of fibre-optic light above

the bar and, along the catwalk, androids who first drew breath at the Mutoid Waste Company. Equally

Fabio invites you to enter an imaginary landscape that offers a palette of sensory teasers rather than a single narrative. Here lurks a whole collection of stories waiting to be discovered

fascinating are illuminated plastics at the Hong Kong outlet of Anna Molinari - Blumarine. The man is more than simply another prestigious Italian export. This is a unique voice capable of being heard over the cacophony of contemporary design.

We first met at Fabio's place on the outskirts of Milan: a space in which he both lives and works. Sunshine pouring through large industrial windows pooled on the grey concrete floor. I spotted a king-size bed tucked away behind a partition. More conspicuous were a couple of drawing tables beneath the windows, stacked loudspeakers, a Fender and some pretty freaky furniture. The working-living quarters of this urban nomad respond to the same criterion that applies to Novembre the designer: Live your life like a work of art. A pillow bearing an image of Fabio sporting a crown of fibre-optic thorns and the message 'Be Your Own Messiah' is not blasphemy but a supreme expression of self-confidence. It is not a written statement of belief but a visual manifesto inspired by the work of men like Joe Colombo, Verner Panton and Carlo Mollino. Let's get rid of the pompously serious statements spewed by so many in the design business, it seems to say, and express our love for humanity. Love and fun and nothing else.

There is an undeniably spiritual dimension to Fabio's work. Like many of Italy's god-fearing atheists, he puts existential issues above a desire for postindustrial prosperity unrelated to personal responsibility. Although he envisions new utopias, they are not the dream worlds of perfection that characterise modernism. His concept has more in common with Shakespeare's fairytale settings and Calvino's Invisible Cities. Myth takes precedence over progress, and modernism, relegated to the past, ends up as the opposite of what it promised to be: a new form of classicism trapped in a neo-baroque period. A bit of nostalgia for a paradise that failed to materialise.

Where does Fabio look for inspiration? The most obvious source is the female body. Soft and supple curves flow through all his designs, and he doesn't deny their origin. His poetic attempt to convince the owners of the Atlantique to hire him was a yearning ode to femininity: 'Architecture is like a beautiful woman – you want her nude, sculptural in her most intimate and structural forms, perfectly true like a picture by Helmut Newton, with a fierce cried-out sexuality.' But I'm sure that the year of his birth, 1966, is an equally magical source of inspiration. That was the year that the Hochschule für Gestaltung in Ulm closed its doors, unable to cope with a burgeoning consumer society. Venturi learned from Las Vegas in anticipation of publishing the results of his research in the early seventies. Andy Warhol filmed the Velvet Underground. Archizoom and Superstudio energised the architectural scene. In London, Peter Cook and his amazing Archigram group promoted a high-tech approach that would 'inject noise into the system'. So much of the radical spirit of the sixties – a decade that shouted 'full speed ahead' – is alive in Fabio's work. He may have missed experiencing the sixties as an adult, but his designs are a reincarnation of his infancy.

Novembre sees his search for totality in art, for nonlinear versatility and for ornament as an altruistic grace as a mandatory coping mechanism for dealing with the problems posed by a technology-driven consumer society. He's out to create visual narratives that do not necessarily reduce the complexity of our lives but that do add a new dimension to what we see. Without disregarding the details of his projects, Fabio restores old with new and mixes mass-produced and handcrafted materials. His designs are more than an answer to our craving for the unique. Saddened by the increasing dearth of quality and lack of concern around him, he says that rather than a design with no precedent, what matters is a design that rewards the observer with a lasting impression – one that offers the user a new way of looking at his surroundings. He's describing a theme that has been vital to Italian design for ages, a concept that lies at the very heart of Italy's epic history of design. At the same time, however, Fabio readily accepts the code of individualism that emerged in the sixties and remains firmly implanted in our society today. He deals with the mass-industrial aspect of contemporary culture by rejecting collective solutions. People who want more freedom, he says, have to be ready to take more personal responsibility. Such a conviction implies that aesthetic values cannot be separated from ethical concerns. Don't look for spiritual and emotional fulfilment in an ugly environment. You won't find it. Listen to your heart. Stop talking about a better world and get to work. Just do it, whether or not you can afford the shoes that go with the slogan. Being a true progettista, Fabio believes that professional titles are irrelevant. Man himself is art. Life is creativity. Transforming one's work into an expressive medium is a highly personal challenge.

Surprisingly, Novembre is not a master at the drawing board. His preferred tool of trade is the written or spoken word. This 'handicap' has no negative effect on his work, however. He's a firm believer in the energy of place and in the power of imagination. Looking for a vision, he listens to the ambience. He refers to architecture, his medium of choice, as the ultimate challenge of three-dimensionality, the last medium to acknowledge that human beings are made of flesh and blood and to recognise that, ultimately, we are all that exists. The spaces that he creates are little gems scattered across the cityscape: jewels that stir emotion, neon shrines that spark passion, zones that trigger contemplation.

Fabio's hot pursuit of sex is fuelled, at least in part, by the rationale that led Ettore Sottsass to say that

existence is a sensory rather than a mental experience. Sottsass was obviously referring to far more than the

idea of a Casanova lost among the courtesans of Venice: a perpetually unsatisfied man wandering the streets

of a medieval city, unable to reconcile the desires of mind and body. Trying to analyse Novembre's visual

messages, I wonder if his 'dream to top all dreams' might not be the ability to fathom the powers of man and

nature, a desire expressed by another Shakespearean character: Prospero, exile of The Tempest. I see in

Fabio's work the wish to love, unencumbered by a need for technologies that tame, obscure and kill innate

human passion. Each of his projects attempts to capture all our senses, to express emotion in a single

gesture, to evoke images of the past, to convey desire and to probe the depths of human nature. Even though

I may be missing an essential factor or two, I know that tenderness is an unmistakable part of what he is and

does. Poetry, in every sense of the word, defines the man. Poems are the building blocks of Novembre's

architecture, and every block is a moving composition in free verse.

Preoccupied with the sensory qualities of
his creations, Novembre doesn't give a
damn about what other designers think.
He's oblivious to styles, movements
and manifestos

Having trained to be a mechanic, Leo Gullbring (1959, Stockholm) went on to broaden his horizons at the University of
Stockholm and the University of Lund, where he studied the history of economics, the philosophy of science and semiotics.
Currently working as a journalist and photographer, the versatile Swede brings his unique slant on architecture and design to
the pages of Scandinavian magazines and dailies such as Göteborgsposten, Area, Form (all published in Sweden) and
Nordisk Interiör (Norway). Gullbring is a contributing editor to Frame and a cultural reporter – again specialising in the areas
of architecture and design – for the Swedish Broadcasting Service.

I speak no facts, I tell tales...

dreams are true,
not memories.

Even the floor gets an eyeful of every move you make.

Anna Molinari
Blumarine Shop
Hong Kong

Architecture is like a beautiful woman – it should be nude, sculptural in
its innermost structural forms, perfectly true, and filled with the self-
confidence of explicit sexuality. But the open senses of contemporary
nomadic populations experience these sonic influences as fatally magnetic
siren songs, sweet and tragic, seductive and pitiless, drowning dreams
of passionate coitus in the oblivion of metropolitan billows.
Erotic and shipwrecked techno-pop surfers cast away on an archipelago
of indistinct chromatic shadings develop unkempt survival styles in an
after-the-flood range of rainbow hues. Their free-and-easy but effective
approach to design is as unprejudiced as a package of coloured condoms.
This is the architecture of safe sex, of mutual and synchronised orgasmic
heights of amorous ecstasy enjoyed by those who, having been rescued
from the shipwreck, savour the taste of life as if for the first time.
It is the architecture of castaways, of people who have survived the gravity
of structures subjected to collapse and reconstruction, dust and altars –
structures capable of floating in air, cunning and indifferent to the
treacherous whirlwinds of everyday life.
Stateless and godless, agnostic and arrogant, they find themselves singing
with the sirens amongst the abandoned wrecks of a modern industrial age.
Heedless of fixed scores and schemes, they carve space with the instinctive
randomness of the forest explorer, the blows of their machetes applied
with youthful vigour, their attitude courageous but foolhardy.
We are these superficial superheroes, atypical ancestors, filthy fashion
plates, beach-blanket boasters with surfboards and plastic pails, polarising
prisms lolling in the midday sun of the tropics of the soul, on an
archipelago of frequencies from infra-mango to ultra-strawberry, indulging
in propitious bacchanals in a state of intoxicating universal religiosity...
        ...in any case...

...I don't want to talk about tales of the sea,

the bracing salt air, love letters in sand,

kidnappings, pirates or beautiful bods,

gilded mermaids or skin burned red

by sun and salt, love and the sea.

Perpetual motion that all things surrounds

so gently so cruelly rocks you with waves,

and it is your destiny, there were you born,

there will you learn to discern the right path.

With flat boards you fly o'er the crest of the waves

of rhythms and colours, fragrances, flavours,

between air and earth, 'twixt water and flame,

for some all's in earnest, for others a game.

All I know is all this may last years or just hours,

as we try to distinguish passion from pity,

there are those who grab waves and hang on for dear life

while others can tame them to gallop like steeds,

in the end it's no matter who wins, loses, draws,

all are just driftwood washed up on the beach,

on stretches of sand burnt by the sun,

smelling of sea, of love and of salt.

Messages in bottles and flashes in pans

consumed in the space from one wave to the wish

to start over again, to let yourself go,

to dive back to swim in the blue and to learn

that he who hits bottom and he who would float

aren't divided by difference, but only by distance.

And those who would stop on the beach to observe

can do nothing but listen to the tales of the sea.

[FN]

A series of doorways greets visitors and leads to a catwalk where a model lives out every woman's dream to strut her stuff.

Blue velvet curtains are pulled back to reveal a ceiling decorated with light bulbs and glass roses.

Dark desires of feminine passion gather behind every curtain.

Anna Molinari Blumarine Shop Hong Kong

32   A glass façade separates the street from an interior that seems to expand and then diminish in size.
The entrance area features a glass and concrete 'bridge' with built-in lighting.

34   A room completely clad in blue mosaic tile features a tiered ceiling fitted out with neon-blue track lighting. Part of the floor erupts into two mosaic 'volcanoes' spouting glass flowers.

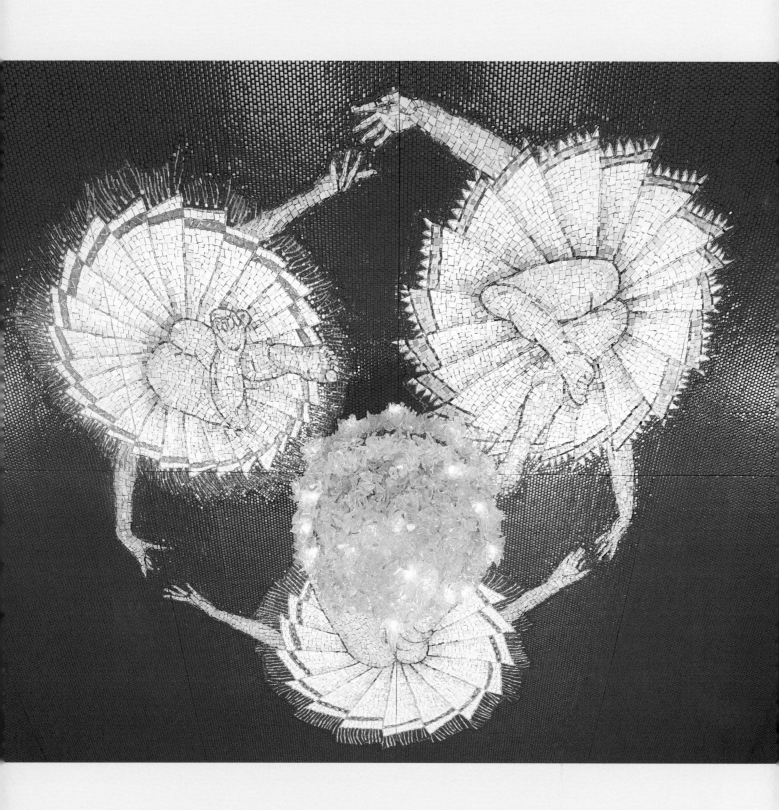

36   Three mosaic dancers spinning around a glass chandelier reveal only arms above and bare bodies below their flying skirts.

37

40 Changing rooms in this shop resemble luxurious padded cells in a private psychiatric hospital for the wealthy.

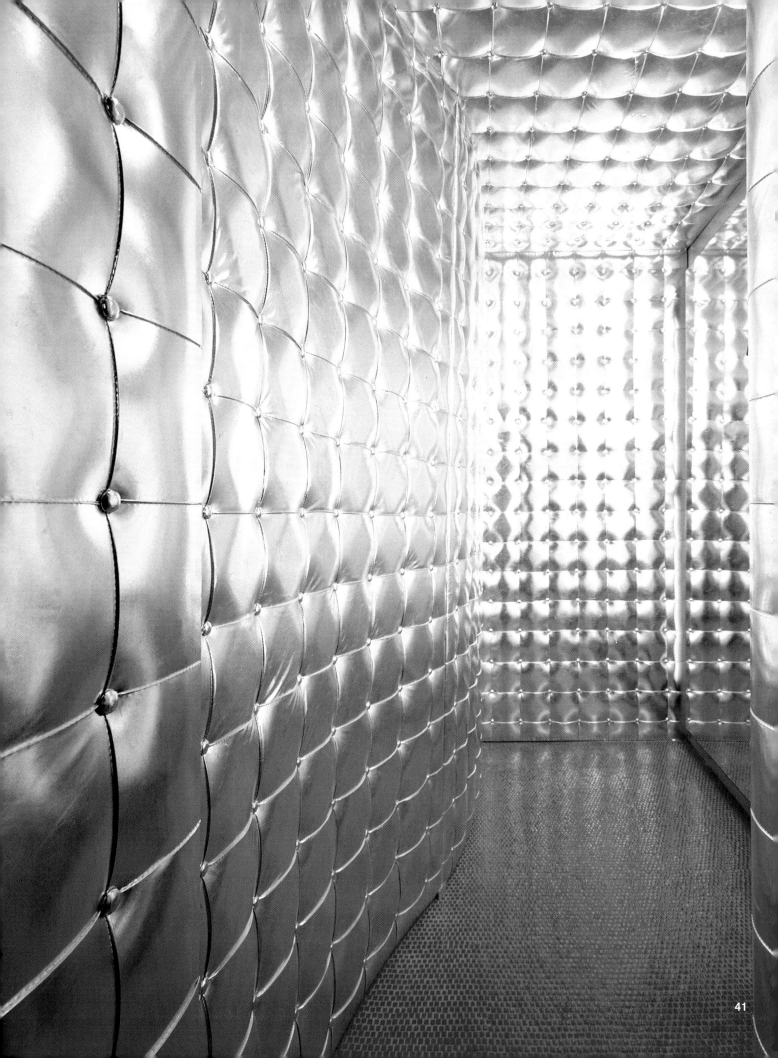

Architects?

They say that we're architects, but what do they mean? They may be saying that we conduct our disciplinary trespassing like cyberspace cowboys, while carefully preserving a procedural ethic, a code of chivalry. The game consists of sitting at the Round Table and constantly shuffling the cards as knights keep assigning arbitrary values and changing the rules. King Arthur taught us that if we're forced to cheat, it's best to keep a straight face. This, too, is important. Knowing what happens in the end is not significant. After all, we can't read the last few pages of an unwritten book. The object may resemble a diary, but no dates are indicated. Everyone morning you pull on a day, like a pair of underwear, to keep your jeans and your life from rubbing against your genitals. They say it makes you sterile. It's true that we have no room for the timelessness that lives inside us. It's true that we have to be quick in this ninja culture of generational survival. One sketch and you're ready. You can't predict the next move, because the goal isn't to put the king in check. Here we go, right past Duchamp, who's seated at a table in Washington Square. The king does not exist. King Arthur exists, of course, but that's another story. So the castle moves diagonally, surprising the bishop in the act of attempting a frontal attack, and the knight leaps off the chessboard, galloping in pursuit of the shadow on the floor, cast by a cloud. He runs into Mollino, followed by Kuramata, and in the heat of the moment crashes into a group of rationalist rooms heaped on top of an architecture manual that topples noisily to the ground. The knight doesn't turn in the saddle to watch. What's done is done. But in that moment he wonders who the first two figures were. He doesn't know, and he regrets his ignorance. We do know. It's quite evident. Every man has his own story, and so does every cloud. The clouds you see today resemble those you saw yesterday. Or do they? Are they the same colour? Not really. Let's hope it rains, at least. Oh. It's already raining.

[FN]

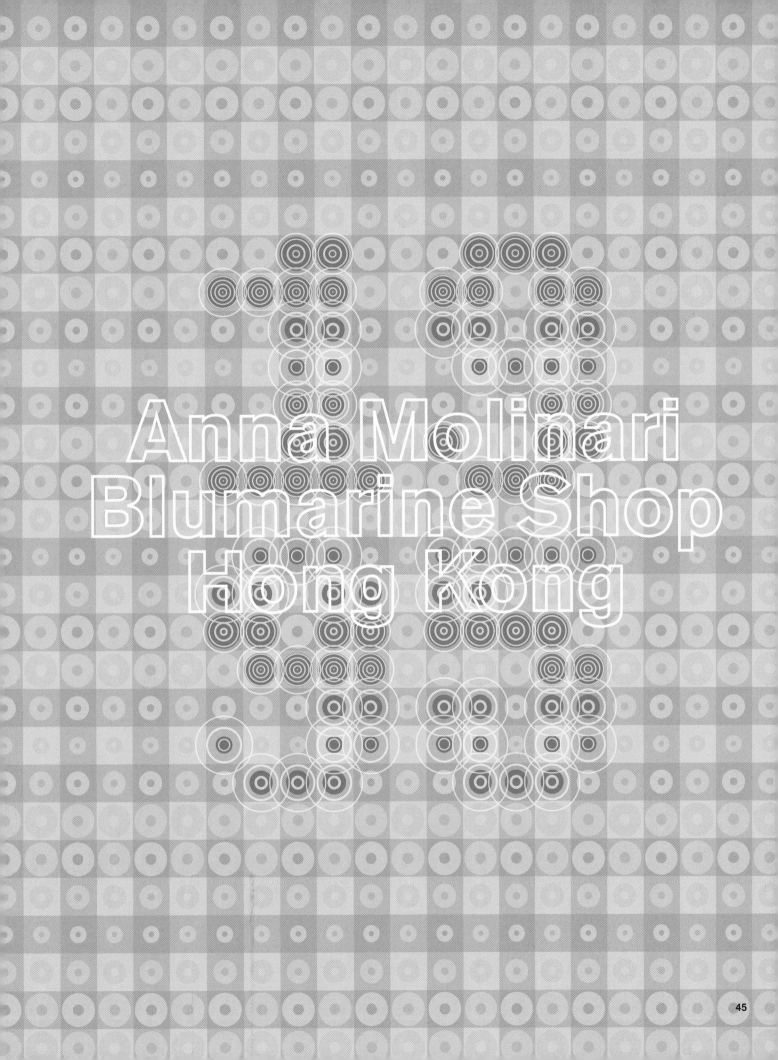

Anna Molinari
Blumarine Shop
Hong Kong

46   The heart of the space is a shining column sheathed in gold leaf and topped by a huge suspended disc studded with light bulbs and glass roses in various colours. Alternating bands of black and white carpet radiate from this point and influence the rest of the design.

The sofa surrounding the column faces changing rooms organised concentrically like drop curtains for the perfect performance.

48   Three existing columns are concealed inside a voluptuous torso clad in pink Lycra and illuminated from within.

L'Atlantique Bar-Restaurant Milan

Love Grows on Sex

Bored to death with bow and arrow, Cupid flew

into Milan in 1995 and bought a laser gun.

There, in a deconsecrated industrial cathedral,

a once masculine structure took on a gentle,

celestial quality as the feminine desire to

rebalance an existing organicist environment

began to erode spatial intimacy. Compression,

followed by expansion, catapulted metropolitan

castaways into unforeseen oceans, and an atoll,

interrupted at the moment of explosion, became

a port of call. A language of shattered crystal

shored up by caryatids offered warm beaches

of yellow flames reaching to the sky. Perhaps it

was love as, from the height of ocean terraces,

huge daisies shed their leaves. Sex was a certainty

in view of intimate parts painted blue and

Bordeaux red in boudoir style. While silhouettes

evoked memories, a television screen crackled with

a succession of images, encouraged by a muezzin

beating out the rhythm of modern prayer from a

coastal tower. Ancient Chinese wisdom embedded

in the steel environment of the garden was to be

the ideogrammatic solution to this spatial enigma:

love grows on sex.

[FN]

54   Beneath a fibre-optic chandelier, the central bar rises like a steel island afloat in a light-showered sea of blue mosaic:
a refuge for castaways.

A low wall encloses a tiered area in which the daisy theme is expressed as a decorative motif on seats, fibreglass wall lamps and mosaic flooring.

57

Nuovamente Exhibition on Recycling Milan

A Good Serpent

Timothy Leary said, 'Maximum freedom should mean maximum responsibility.' Any consideration of recycling should be filtered through Leary's intuition. The freedom we pursue navigates in the living flux of experience, in the wake of a sense of cosmic belonging. It can be found in the harmony between the individual microcosm and the planetary macrocosm. The level of responsibility necessary to achieve freedom is like a surfboard on the crest of a wave of expanding human energy, a discovery and an optimisation of the vitality that marks the incessantly precarious ecological equilibrium between planet and species. The surfer awakens in a crisis of logic and analytical thought brought about through the magic of falling in love. The technique of persuasion is cancelled out by pervasive flashes of lightning that playfully close the production cycle in a merry-go-round of futile but free and perfect creations.

Once upon a time there was a good serpent named UROBOROS, who to avoid hurting anyone fed on his own tail, drawing the energy he required to live from his own body. UROBOROS lived near a village populated by people who, surely unaware of Buddhist and Judeo-Christian stories, felt great affection for UROBOROS and had no preconceptions about snakes. The children dreamed of growing tall so they could reach up and pat UROBOROS, who remained suspended between earth and sky. Men in the village knew nothing but the curved lines of the snake's coils and the bodies of women, and this is how they built their houses. The houses resembled one another in form but were different in appearance, just like human beings. The interior of each house was as free and light as the flight of the thoughts that lived there.

And they all lived happily ever after.

[FN]

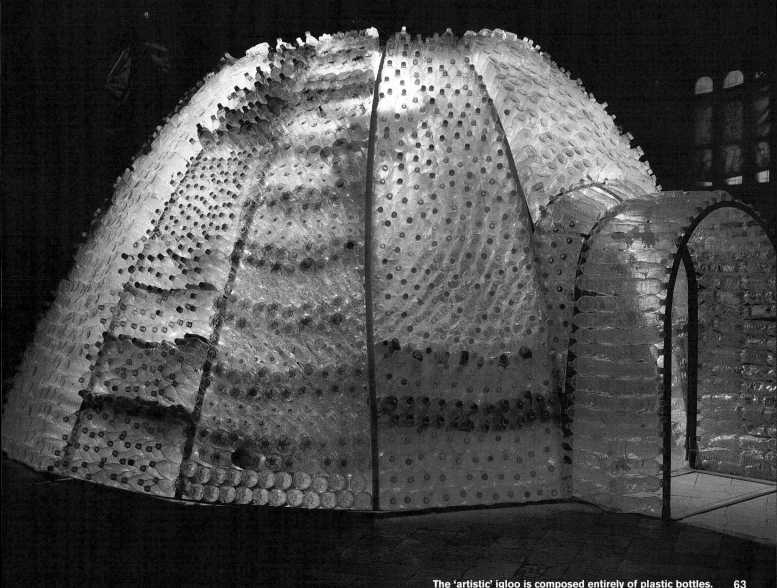

The 'artistic' igloo is composed entirely of plastic bottles. 63

64   A view from the entrance shows the head and tail of a suspended snake in the foreground. The snake's body
      – made of cellophane wound around suspended rings – is inflated by an industrial fan located inside the mouth.

An igloo based on a mechanical theme is made of car parts and acrylic sheeting.

The interior surface of the 'domestic' igloo is lined in Tetra Pak.

Fluorescent acrylic display columns are provided with built-in lighting.

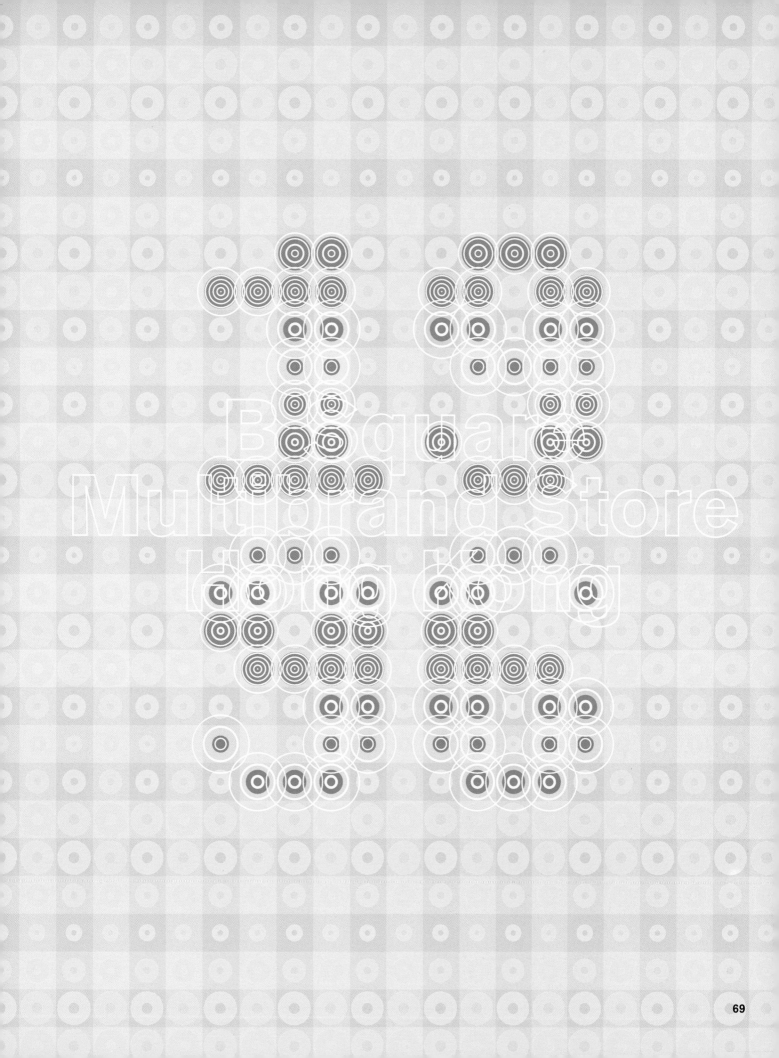

70   Acrylic niches interrupt the steel wall leading to the changing rooms, where acrylic doors reiterate the colour scheme.

A silver ceiling in the display area features exposed pipes and wiring.

You Are
Breathing

You are breathing. Are you aware of it? Breathing
is the invisible umbilical cord that connects us to
the earth. Every one of us, without exception.
At the geometric centre of your body is a thing
called a belly button. First you were nourished
through it as you floated in a warm maternal bath.
But now it's a scar, a memory. Now you breathe air.
And if you run out of breath as you chop down
a tree, don't blame it on the tree.

[FN]

ON – Natural Wellness Center Milan

78   The staircase to the floor below follows the line of the drop ceiling, which provides space for all wiring.
Steel-framed heating grids are next to the banisters.

The ceiling continues along a corridor lined, on one side, by illuminated panels of obscure glass which serve an aesthetic function. Access to toilets is at the far end of the corridor.

Reflections from aluminium and black resin surfaces distort and magnify spatial perception.

Music in 3D

The project requires the help of workers and craftsmen to coordinate and conduct it as they would a symphony orchestra. This is a soundless music whose efficacy will continue over time for unconsciously aware audiences. Perhaps the relationship between music and the use of architecture is connected to the concept. Goethe defined architecture as 'congealed music', but I like to think of it as something solidly mounted on sound tracks that meander through the various moments that make up every day of our lives. The music of architecture beats the rhythm of the heart. It is registered in thoughts, superimposed on images and mingled in flavours. This is music to drink, to eat, to ease acquaintance and to accompany lovemaking. The real function of public places is to soothe the solitude of private life. Paul Valery said that a man alone is in bad company. I like to imagine myself as a strategic Cupid for encounters and love affairs that happen in the places I design. All my projects to date have been designed for the public, a fact that makes me happy, because I believe in architecture as a multiplier of energy. I also believe in lively interaction between a space and its users. 'In architecture, coitus is the void,' said Elemire Zolla, and I like seeing that void full of people exchanging emotions and consuming passions.

[FN]

Blu
Disco
Lodi

Monochromatic Filter

Blu is a leap in the dark, an immersion in apnoea. It is an obsession born of the idea of viewing things through a monochromatic filter. It is a single-frequency abstraction pulsating on bodies in free movement. Beads of blue silicone illuminate white vinyl sofas from Edra, and the steel central bar stands out against this backdrop like a ship run aground. Stroboscopic UFOs created by Gianluca Sbrana dance in suspension. Light filters through a plaster drop ceiling clad in fluorescent paint, causing Tom Dixon's phosphorescent Jacks to sparkle. Hemispheric mirrors punctuate the surface of the walls, attacked by streams of light that disintegrate into a thousand light particles. A work that street poet Silvestro Sentiero dedicated to designer Fabio Novembre forms a guardrail: 'Show me the freedom of swallows.'

[FN]

The steel structure at the rear of the bar and, in the private area, a surface featuring the ends of metal pipes   87
mark the route to the dance floor.

88   **Guardrails are the metal letters of a poem, hemispheric mirrors on the walls are stars in a night sky, and white seats float in a blue sea of relaxation.**

A view of the private area and the central bar features stroboscopic chandeliers.

A structure atop the ticket office radiates a conical 'spray' of blue neon light.

Beads of blue silicone send a shower of light onto white vinyl sofas.

Light and Shadow

I'm interested in light as a carrier of shadow. The occidental idea of darkness as the absence of light seems quite sterile when compared with the oriental concept, which attributes the same value to both qualities. Perfect transparency, the legacy of Judeo-Christian prophecy, meets its ideal light at the point of zenithal saturation. What I try to recreate in my work is a mutable theatre of shadows, the offspring of mystical opacity. I live in the present. I do not miss oil lamps. Flashes of neon hypnotise me just as much as the flames in a fireplace do. In my eyes, electro-luminescence has the same intensity as burning coals, and fibre optics enhances the potential inherent in traditional candlelight. Modernity widens the horizons of possibility in pursuit of the conceivable.

Power to the imagination!

[FN]

To get in, visitors use their bodies to cancel the book-cover barcode that envelops the entrance area.
For those unfamiliar with South of Memphis, this is a chance to get acquainted with another of Novembre's creations.

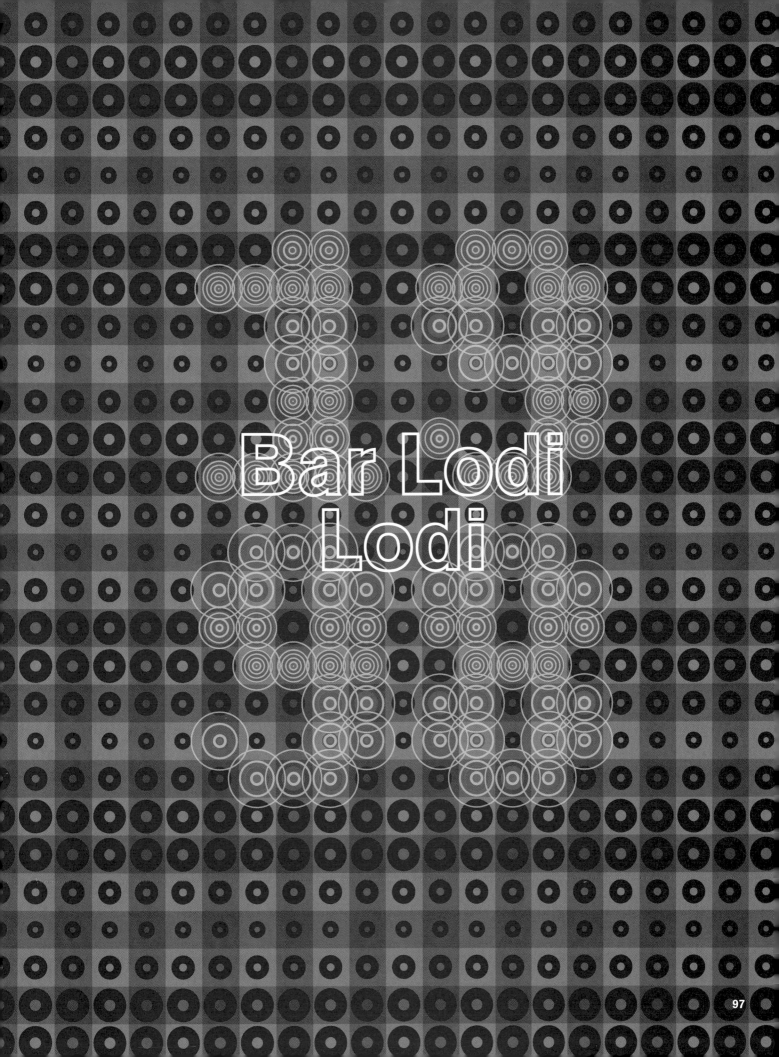

Bar Lodi
Lodi

Evidence

Ingredients

The Factory, N.Y.C., 1969

The Book, Milan, 1995

The Bar, Lodi, 1998

People, words, places: adequate but unnecessary conditions for a controversial and personal recipe for architecture. Ladies and gentlemen: meet Novembre at the lounge in Lodi. A tunnel and an enforced crossing axis are the given conditions. Spatial magnification and a functional sequence are the solutions proposed.

Instructions for use

Use your body to cancel the book-cover barcode that envelops the entrance hall. Proceed to a tunnel lined with illuminated Factory components whose shadowy silhouettes, artificially projected on the ground, act as an organic barcode to scan your entrance. If you want a drink, approach the slab that runs the length of the tunnel and place your order. Warhol's shadow beneath your feet indicates the end of the tunnel. Change directions and, drink in hand, find a resting place on suspended discs that fill the background space and offer a trompe l'oeil perspective, along with intermittent glimpses of the piazza.

The Factory appears in a photograph by Richard Avedon, New York, 1969.

The Book is *South of Memphis* by Fabio Novembre, Idea Books, Milan, 1995.

The Bar is at 25 Piazza della Vittoria, Lodi, 1998.

[FN]

Silhouettes 'cut out' of the mirrored wall produce artificial shadows on the mosaic floor.   101

The book-cover barcode, when inverted, lends access to a table and seating area at the other end of the bar.

104   The mirrored wall facing the bar magnifies the space. A glossy steel door leads to the toilets.

Via Spiga
Showroom
Milan

Zen Baroque

Shoes rest on shelves a mere step away from me. Everything seems to indicate that people are coming to reclaim their footwear, to let these shoes take them away from this place. Am I viewing part of a ritual that includes a multitude of objects and implies a multitude of people? Judging by what they wear, each person is different. I wonder if the young woman who took off her little red shoes is involved with the gentleman who's left his white loafers on the shelf. Does the owner of the black handbag also wear those ebony boots? In my mind I see faces, hear names, inhale scents and listen to stories, some of which intersect with my own narrative, spinning only a breath away. The golden envelope surrounding this space creates a strain of baroque music from the score of a Zen garden. The sound of my steps on the wooden walkway cuts through the peaceful silence. Surely I'm standing in the vestibule of a sacred place, a temple in which feet are like table legs, rooted to the ground. He who returns to this spot recognises the shoes he removed before pausing to meditate. Watch as he slips them on and walks away.

[FN]

A window onto the forecourt offers a view inside.

A uniting element is the ascending wooden walkway that defines the transecting axis of the space.   115

Steps lead to a wooden walkway.

Curved plaster walls ornamented with gold leaf conceal devices used to attach projecting glass shelves to the walls.

Chez Moi

Cooking is the only genteel way to penetrate hungry bodies. Generosity is expressed through the quality of being available to others, a characteristic that transcends good culinary practices. You end up voluntarily offering yourself as an object of cannibalism. You become a speciality served at ritual feasts or in corporate cafeterias, a delicacy often unknowingly consumed but necessary and inevitable for the continuation of the species. Morsels of self are your attempt to fill the stomach with food for the soul. In a nutshell, you have to let yourself be eaten.

[FN]

Shu
Bar-Restaurant
Milan

122 **The bar is a silver spaceship that emits a green neon light. The structure of the bar moderates and progressively reduces the height of the environment: a strategy created to attract patrons.**

Separated from the walls by the perimeter of the room, the sloping trapezoid drop ceiling resembles a printed circuit diagram.   125

126   Walls made of safety glass are peppered with pistol shots and illuminated around the edges.

Chip-studded circuit boards are featured on light boxes mounted on the ceiling.

Transparent Reflections

Reflect beneath a hemispheric vault, a cranial skylight, a semitransparent firmament. Watch as the reflection spreads. Semitransparency eludes Manichaeism. A frosted glass filters existential nudity and restores the power of the imagination. Intentionally out of focus, the vision trespasses on the territory of dreams, in which anything is possible. Who can say that the shadows, quick and agile, are without a life of their own? That they are unable to balance out luminous arrogance? They follow us of their own free will, playing changing roles in different situations, acting as protectors, intimidators, inspirers or decorative extras in a bright, improvised dance around the flame of our very flesh. We dare to defy the darkness with incandescent resistance, and wherever the energy is less, fellowship increases, as does the presence of shadows.

[FN]

130   Two mosaic-clad alcoves with built-in lighting accommodate the telecommunications zone.

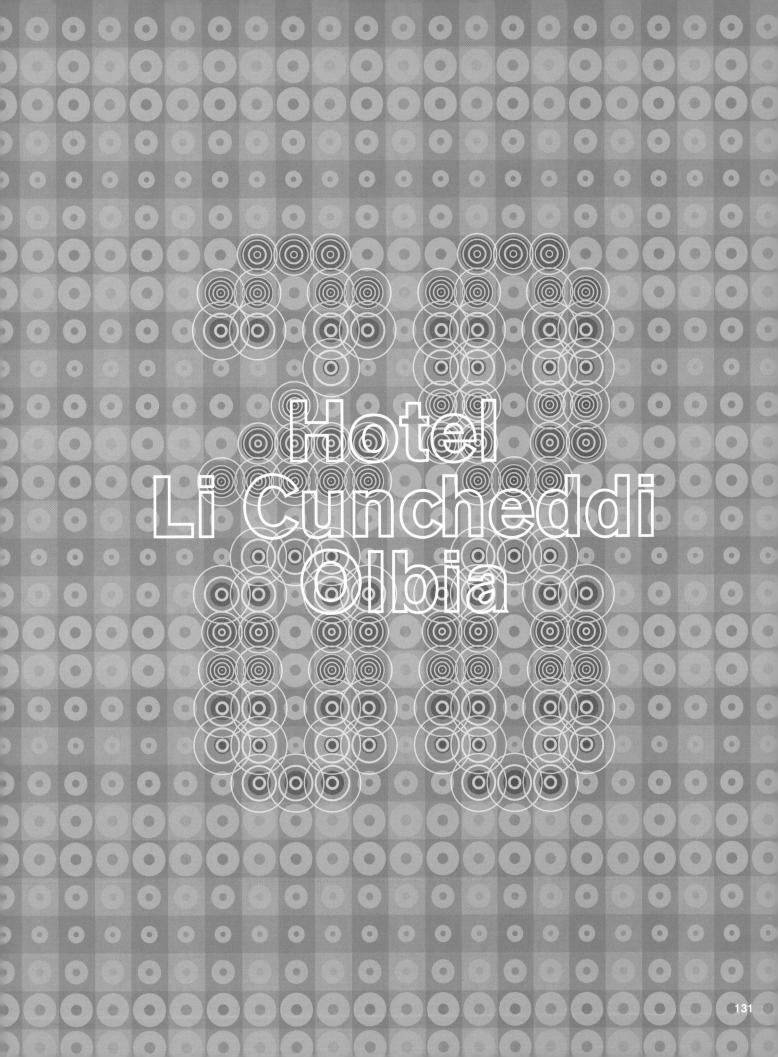

Hotel
Li Cuncheddi
Olbia

132   The reception to the right of the entrance is contained in a longitudinal recess within the curved foyer area.

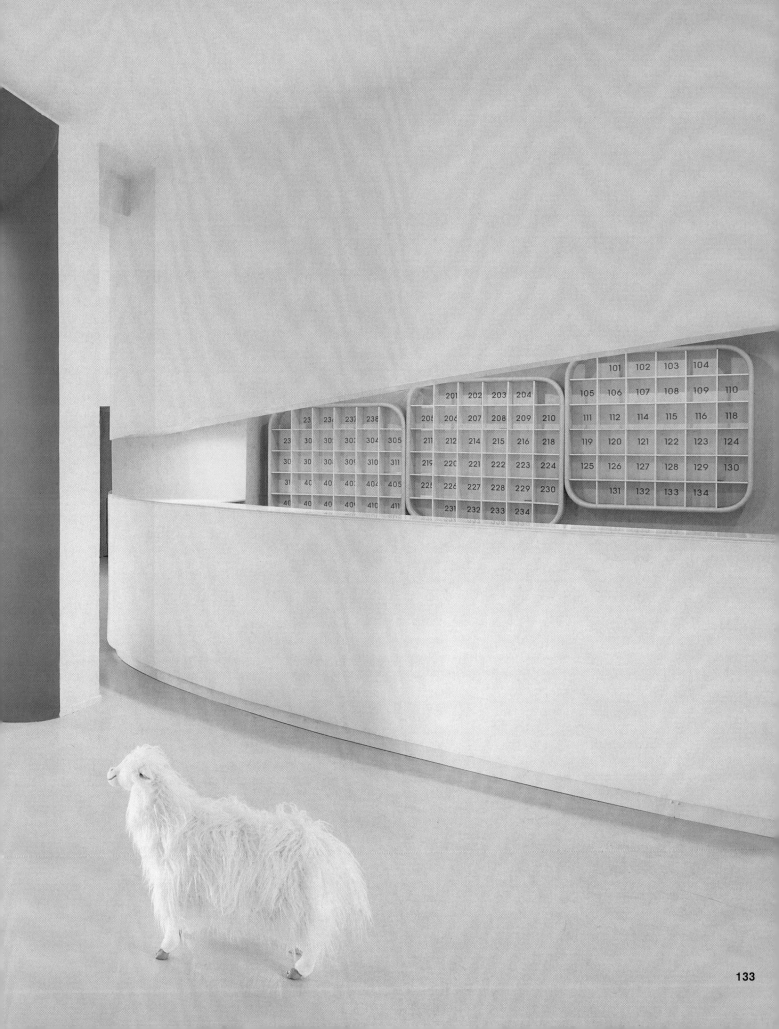

A central bar incorporating two different structures features tiered seating that offers a view of the outdoor surroundings.   135

Yellow recesses in the curved walls serve as shelves and directional signs in the night zone.

An existing column transformed into a large rattan-covered totem keeps a watchful eye on people moving through the foyer.

A steel window frame turns the view outside into a picture postcard.

Mirrored surfaces above the bridge-like structure of the bed seem to expand the existing space.

To Become or to Grow Into

Rollerblades are the only way to get a physical idea of the difference between becoming and growing into. Let me explain. In the Italian language, the two terms are seen as synonyms, but as often happens, it is best to go beyond the dictionary definition and try to sense the meaning that a word evokes. If I close my eyes, becoming seems like walking, a process that involves a sequence of steps that may vary in speed but that always relate to a binary condition required by the action. To grow into, on the other hand, makes me think of a smooth and sliding unitary motion. As for Rollerblades, putting them on leads to a perfect demonstration of the clumsy movements that simple bipeds can make on a smooth surface. Skimming along on aligned, perfectly oiled wheels – slipping over the world with an agility that seemingly transcends the evolution of the species – is vivid evidence of man's innate capacity to improve on the conditions imposed. I reached this conclusion when I saw the exhibition on Piero Manzoni at Palazzo Reale in Milan. I stood on his pedestal sculpture, which features two inviting shoeprints, and thought that had he been alive today, surely Manzoni would have opted for indentations made by Rollerblades. In any case, I believe in the 'stargate', in molecular transport, in a leap into hyperspace. Some distances can never be spanned by a logical, step-by-step approach. There are sudden leaps – momentary losses of reference that correspond to the great innovations of man – in which pure intuition of the kind that verges on madness sweeps away the logic of gradual progress.

[FN]

Bisazza Stand
Cersaie
Bologna

Taking Flight

I've never been able to assign myself coordinates, especially when it comes to the rigid system of Cartesian axes. And when I'm told to toe the line – the straight and narrow path so overrated in Western culture – I become a slalom racer, an authority on curves and smooth bends. Nevertheless, I am fully aware of the vacuity of the vortex and of the need to transform its narcissism into a state of flux. But only by forgetting Euclidean geometry and subsequent attempts to tile over the world can I hope to take flight. Like winged fish out of water who rise to the sky and flock together, pieces in an Escher-like puzzle emerge from an ideal RGB system of a cathode-ray tube and pour into monochrome beds, between banks of coherent matter and along paths that defy the perception of gravity and lead to random encounters.

By the way, did a certain Mr. Tatlin happen to call?

[FN]

For Sale

Let's not mince words: to survive you have to transform needs into desires.

The (trans)formation of needs into desires is a stage on which to play out the developments of a saturated market. Supply is much greater than demand, or, to put it more simply, there are a lot more chairs out there than there are backsides. Therefore the credit for selling more chairs to the same backsides goes to he who sells, not to he who produces or he who designs. And the percentage of profit pocketed by he who sells a finished product is from five to twenty times greater than the quota assigned to 'artistic' merit. If we look at the situation from another point of view, the sale is the only safety valve for an accumulation of merchandise that is becoming an economic burden and a cause of unemployment. Consequently, the sale remains the indispensable link in the chain that seals the gates of that private reserve where the old brontosauruses of capitalism graze, with their demiurgic notion of the project: the unlimited exploitation of resources. It's becoming increasingly clear that such a production cycle is no longer compatible with an ecosystem of consumption suitable for planet Earth. But do pushers worry about curing the bad habits of their customers? No one ever 'lays in some supplies' any more, with an eye to survival; everyone is too busy 'shopping', an English word that has been adopted by cultures all over the world – the gerund of the noun 'shop', which is a place designated for the sale of various products. A shop is a communicatory interface between production and consumption. The role of supply is to seduce, to charm, and the shop is a point of contact and relation. The stimulation of desires through sensory perceptions offered within a retail space draws users towards what is now called 'aesthetic consumption'. The race is on. Behold the invention of dreams made to measure and, for the hearing-impaired and others in need of further explanation, translations and subtitles to clarify the din of flirtatious beckoning transmitted through advertising. To be a consumer and to exert the power of the purchase: these are the fundamental principles of the democracy of consumption, the constitutional rights of the republic of capitalism and the third-world aspirations of those in search of a better life. Hypocritical moralising aside, however, self-determination is the only fundamental tenet here. From legalised drugs to free porno, toleration is the word. The resemblance between a line of people waiting for food in Rwanda and a line outside a Prada shop before a big sale can be interpreted only in terms of the indefiniteness of the principle of necessity.

My signature is Fabio Novembre, I'm a creator of shops, which I use as empty pages on which to write my stories. A fast-paced schedule is of the essence, and my strategies are impossible to explain, as is the idea of the architecture that allegedly supports them. My shops have been accused of grandstanding, of overwhelming the products on display. Clients insist that I accept walk-on parts to sustain the operation. But they keep on giving me work. The only real freedom I grant to those who enter my shops is to buy or not to buy. That's it.

[FN]

On the ground floor, a mosaic surface rises through the space like an erect spine.

Displays made of acrylic ride the spine of a mosaic surface, which resembles the skin of a crocodile.

The meticulously made display cases can be locked. 163

View of the basement and the ground floor. A mirror-clad ceiling makes the play with horizontal and vertical lines even stronger.

166   In the basement, the Policor cladding of the floor rises here and there to display shoes and leather accessories.

Neanderthal Design?

Rampant neo-primitivism.

Artist's shit.

Telematic synthesis?

Existential dispersal?

Loss of centre.

A different tradition.

Axis mundi.

Holy place: point of rupture in the homogeneity of space.

Cannibalism: cultural behaviour based on a religious vision of life.

Cult of the dead or death of the cult?

Living persons but destined to die.

Desanctification of human existence?

Disguised mythology?

Degrading ritualism?

Pissing in one's own mouth.

Farewell ideological project: because cynical man requires less difficult things.

Ground xerox of culture.

Religion and mythology hidden in the shadows of the unconscious.

Neanderthal.

Menhir.

All you can know is that they exist.

So be it.

Jean Baudrillard, Alighiero Boetti, Daniel Defoe, Vincent Wilde, Mircea Levi,

Piero Manzoni, Alessandro Mendini, Hans Sedlmayr.

Thanks to all.

[FN]

Project Credits

Project	Anna Molinari - Blumarine (clothing shop)
Location	R 135, The Regent Arcade, Kowloon, Hong Kong
Client	Anna Molinari
Architect	Fabio Novembre
General contractor	East Joint Limited
Photography	Guy Bertrand
Start design	April 1994
Open for business	June 1994
Seating	Soshun (Edra)
Seating fabric	Velvet
Floor covering	Shiny black concrete with gold mosaic stripes (Bisazza)
Lighting fixtures	Light bulbs
Windows/glass	Curved glass with liquid-crystal display for fitting-room wall
Accessories	Roses of blown glass (Componenti Donà)
Custom furnishings	East Joint Limited

Project	Anna Molinari - Blumarine (clothing shop)
Location	11a Old Bond Street, London, UK
Client	Anna Molinari
Architect	Fabio Novembre
General contractor	GMW Partnership
Photography	Alberto Ferrero
Total surface area	70 square metres
Start design	May 1994
Open for business	September 1994
Seating	Tatlin (Edra)
System furnishings	Padded fitting-room walls (Arnaboldi & Riva s.n.c.)
Floor covering	Mosaic (Bisazza)
Lighting fixtures	Chandelier by Deborah Thomas
Wall covering	Mosaic (Bisazza)
Ceilings	Artwork by Izhar Patkin

Project	Anna Molinari - Blumarine (clothing shop)
Location	Landmark, Hong Kong
Client	Anna Molinari
Architect	Fabio Novembre
General contractor	East Joint Limited
Photography	Guy Bertrand
Start design	December 1994
Open for business	February 1995
Seating fabric	Velvet
System furnishings	Wire-mesh walls framed in stainless steel, with built-in lighting
Floor covering	Carpet
Lighting fixtures	Light bulbs
Surface covering	Central column clad in gold leaf
Accessories	Metal-framed female torso covered in pink Lycra, with built-in lighting; roses in blown glass (Componenti Donà)
Custom furnishings	East Joint Limited

Project	L'Atlantique (bar-restaurant)
Location	42 Viale Umbria, Milan, Italy
Client	Ivano Fatibene
Architect	Fabio Novembre
General contractor	Sinedil
Photography	Alberto Ferrero
Total surface area	1,200 square metres
Start design	November 1994
Open for business	October 1995
Seating	Soshun (Edra), Filina (Edra), baroque armchairs
Tables	GFR
Floor covering	Mosaic (Bisazza)
Lighting fixtures	Chandelier made of optical fibres (Fort Fibre Ottiche)
Surface covering:	Fibreglass-clad columns with built-in lighting (Galli)
Accessories	Manikins (Mutoid Waste Company); large fibreglass daisies with built-in lighting (Galli)
Special component	Video wall (Rent Audio)
Custom furnishings	Italy's Best

Project	Nuovamente (exhibition on recycling)
Location	Palazzo della Ragione, Milan, Italy
Client	AMSA/Replastic/Municipality of Milan
Architect	Fabio Novembre
General contractor	Mutoid Waste Company
Photography	Alberto Ferrero
Start design	September 1996
Open for business	October 1996
Special components	Igloos and snake (Mutoid Waste Company)

Project	B Square (clothing shop)
Location	East Point Road, 24 Sogo New Face, Hong Kong
Client	Bluebell Enterprise Ltd.
Architect	Fabio Novembre
General contractor	East Joint Limited
Photography	Jacky Chee
Total surface area	370 square metres
Start design	September 1996
Open for business	December 1996
System furnishings	Fluorescent acrylic columns with stainless-steel bases and built-in lighting
Floor covering	Concrete floor with stainless-steel joints; certain sections are inlaid with compact discs
Wall covering	Acrylic sheets with built-in lighting
Custom furnishings	East Joint Limited

Project	ON – Natural Wellness Centre
Location	11 Via Podgora, Milan, Italy
Client	Nicola Gurrado
Architect	Fabio Novembre
Design team	Serena Novembre
General contractor	Tecno Beton
Photography	Alberto Ferrero
Total surface area	300 square metres
Start design	May 1996
Open for business	October 1996
Seating	Mattone (Edra)
Floor covering	Epoxy resin
Lighting fixtures	Iodide lights and optical fibres
Wall covering	Oak
Ceilings	Mirrored aluminium panels
Custom furnishings	Italy's Best

Project name	Blu Disco
Location	25 Via Nazioni unite, Lodivecchio, Italy
Client	Antonio Corsano
Architect	Fabio Novembre
Design team	Serena Novembre
General contractor	Rinaldo Bongiorni
Photography	Alberto Ferrero
Total surface area	700 square metres
Start design	February 1996
Open for business	September 1996
Seating	Jack (Eurolounge), Island (Edra)
Lighting fixtures	Illuminated tubes of blue silicone; blue neon
Wall covering	Plaster (G&G di Gualina and Gualtieri)
Ceiling lamps	UFO strobe chandeliers (Gianluca Sbrana)

Project	Bar Lodi
Location	25 Piazza della Vittoria, Lodi, Italy
Client	Antonio Corsano
Architect	Fabio Novembre
Design team	Lorenzo De Nicola, Serena Novembre
General contractor	G&G di Gualina and Gualtieri
Consultants	Graphics: Marco Braga; lighting: Studio Pollice
Photography	Alberto Ferrero
Total surface area	70 square metres
Start design	October 1997
Open for business	June 1998
Seating	R3 (Costantino)
Tables	Chipre (Amat)
Floor covering	Mosaic (Bisazza)
Lighting fixtures	Guzzini, Erco
Wall covering	Mirrored surfaces (Vetro A)
Ceilings	Plaster (G&G di Gualina and Gualtieri)
Custom furnishings	A. Missoni & C

Project	Via Spiga (shoe showroom)
Location	1 Via della Spiga, Milan, Italy
Client	Intershoe s.r.l.
Architect	Fabio Novembre
Design team	Lorenzo De Nicola, Serena Novembre
General contractor	G&G di Gualina and Gualtieri
Photography	Alberto Ferrero
Total surface area	58 square metres
Start design	May 1999
Open for business	September 1999
Seating	S-chair (Cappellini)
Tables	Thomas Roberts
Floor covering	Mosaic (Bisazza) and cedar (T. Roberts)
Lighting fixtures	Zumtobel, Guzzini
Wall covering	Plaster clad in gold leaf
	(G&G di Gualina and Gualtieri)
Ceilings	Plaster (G&G di Gualina and Gualtieri)
Custom furnishings	Almo s.r.l.

Project	Shu (bar-restaurant)
Location	27 Via Crocefisso, Milan, Italy
Client	Molino s.r.l.
Architect	Fabio Novembre
Design team	Lorenzo De Nicola
General contractor	Tecno Beton
Consultants	Graphics: Marco Braga; lighting: Studio Pollice
Photography	Alberto Ferrero
Total surface area	330 square metres
Start design	October 1998
Open for business	June 1999
Seating	La Marie (Kartell), Cariba (Metal Mobil s.r.l.)
Floor covering	Mosaic (Bisazza), epoxy resin (Fabio Carlesso)
Lighting fixtures	Guzzini light boxes in restaurant
	(M. Braga, L. Bertoni and S. Sanfratello)
Wall/surface covering	Black velvet and glass (both rough-edged and
	gunshot) in the restaurant; aluminium
	spray-painted surfaces in the bar
Ceilings	Plaster (ilcri gessi)
Windows/glass	De Rosa Serramenti
Custom furnishings	Almo s.r.l.

Project name	Hotel li Cuncheddi
Location	Capo Ceraso, Olbia, Italy
Client	Nuova Gel s.r.l.
Architect	Fabio Novembre
Design team	Lorenzo De Nicola, Carlo Formisano,
	Etienne Thetard
General contractor	Delta Costruzioni s.n.c
Photography	Alberto Ferrero
Start design	October 1999
Open for business	May 2000
Seating	Gervasoni, Toy (Driade), 3R (Costantino)
Tables	Gervasoni
Floor covering	Mosaic (Bisazza), Pastellone (Collezione Ricordi)
Wall covering	Plaster
Ceiling lamps	Pod Lens (Luceplan), Totem (Gervasoni)
Custom furnishings	Italy's Best, A. Missoni

Project	**Bisazza Stand**
Location	Cersaie 2000, Bologna, Italy
Client	Bisazza s.p.a.
Architect	Fabio Novembre
Design team	Lorenzo De Nicola, Carlo Formisano
General contractor	Expo Stand
Photography	Alberto Ferrero
Total surface area	144 square metres
Start design	September 2000
Floor covering	Logos (Bisazza)
Wall covering	Wood clad in mosaic tile (Bisazza)
Custom furnishings	Expo Stand

Project	**Tardini (leather goods shop)**
Location	142 Wooster Street, New York City, USA
Client	Tarco s.r.l.
Architect	Fabio Novembre
Design team	Marco Braga, Lorenzo De Nicola, Carlo Formisano, Etienne Thetard
Photography	Alberto Ferrero
Total surface area	270 square metres
Start design	December 1999
Open for business	July 2000
Tables	Plexiglas (Neon Color)
System furnishings	Ebony (Almo s.r.l.)
Floor covering	Mosaic (Bisazza); concrete floor (Policor)
Wall covering	Policor (F1 s.r.l.)
Custom furnishings	Almo s.r.l.

Bibliography

Books

Branzaglia, Carlo, ed. *Discodesign in Italy*.
   Edizioni L'Archivolto, Milan, 1996

Gallo, Paola, ed. *New Shops in Italy 4*.
   Edizioni L'Archivolto, Milan, 1997

Gallo, Paola, ed. *New Shops 6: Made in Italy*.
   Edizioni L'Archivolto, Milan, 2000

Gramagna, Giuliana, and Paola Biondi, eds. *Il Design in Italia*.
   Umberto Allemandi & C., Turin, 1999

Lazzaroni, Laura, ed. *35 anni di design 1961-1996 al Salone del*
   Mobile. Edizioni Cosmit, Milan, 1996

Legziel, Elise, ed. *Lo Spettacolo dell'Architettura*.
   Linea Mielle, Milan, 1997

Migliore and Servetto, eds. *New Exhibits 2: Made in Italy*.
   Edizioni L'Archivolto, Milan, 2000

Novembre, Fabio, ed. *A Sud di Memphis*.
   Idea Books Edizioni, Milan, 1995

Seo, Namio, ed. *World Super Interiors*.
   Shotenkenchiku-Sha, Tokyo, 2000

Magazines and Newspapers

2001

Gullbring, Leo. 'Skin City' in *Frame*, January-February, 60-67

Sironi, Fabio. 'Hotel design' in *Carnet*, January, 68+

'Manhattan opening: nel segno del lusso' in *Vogue Pelle*, January, 32

2000

Antonelli, Paola. 'Absolutely Fabio' in *Interiors*, November, cover, 2+

Blokland, Tessa. 'Baroque Zen' in *Frame*, January-February, 12

Blokland, Tessa. 'Heaven and Earth' in *Frame*, March-April, 60-61

Finessi, Beppe. 'Shu, Milano' in *Domus*, May, 54-59

Finessi, Beppe. 'La casa sono io' in *Abitare*, April, 136-141

Gronli, Espen. 'Absolutt Fabios' in *Henne Interior*, February-March, 42-49

Gullbring, Leo. 'Sensuell arkitektur' in *Nordisk Interior*, March, cover,
   13+

Marcos, Pilar. 'La coherencia excéntrica' in *Diseño Interior*, June, 88-89

Mendini, Alessandro. 'Crocoloop' in *Abitare*, December, 154-159

Mutti, Roberta. 'Bagni come architetture' in *Interni Annual Bagno*,
   October, cover, 42+

Padovani, Maddalena. 'Seduzioni silenziose' in *Interni*, October, 97+

Rodermond, Janny. 'Architectonische evenementen van Fabio Novembre'
   De Architect Interieur, May, 52-57

Rodriguez Marcos, Javier. 'Una selecciòn mitica, del minimalismo al easy
   living' in *Diseño Interior*, October, 85.

Soul, Ana. 'Sognando New York' in *Io Donna*, November, 294-303

Vercelloni, Matteo. 'Mare, monti' in *Interni Panorama*, November, 19-21

Vercelloni, Matteo. 'Bar Shu' in *Interni Panorama*, October, 23-24

Vullierme, Lucie. 'Bar à Lodi' in *AMC*, April, 87+

'Restaurante Shu en Milàn' in *Diseño Interior*, July, 126 – 133

'Fabio Novembre' in *Pen*, November, 65

1999

Alfano Miglietti, Francesca. 'Fabio Novembre' in *Virus*,
   June-July-August, 36-39

Bondioli, Chiara. 'Tutti pazzi per Fabio, artista-messia' in Gulliver,
   October, 12

Briatore, Virginio. 'Lo specchio e le sue ombre' in *Interni*, June, 66-69

Briatore, Virginio. 'Il bar del Cappellaio matto' in *Interni Panorama*,
   May, 24-25

Busenkell, Michaela. 'Bar-Code' in *AIT*, June, 6+

Cohen, Edie. 'La Vita Lodi' in *Interior Design*, October, 164-167

Coz, Lauretta. 'Parola d'ordine: Fusion' in *Capital*, December, 302-305

D'Amico, Alberto. 'I negozi come gli spot' in *Italia Oggi*, October, 19-20

Gullbring, Leo. 'Be Your Own Messiah' in *Frame*, July-August, 84-91.

Kroucharska, Margarita. 'Ombre illuminate' in *Neon*,
   September-October, cover, 52-59

Kroucharska, Margarita. 'Il mestiere di vivere' in *Neon*,
   November-December, cover, 46-55

Mancinelli, Antonio. 'Fabio Novembre: spazio ai sentimenti' in *Donna*,
December,120-122

Mattsson, Jay. 'Absolutely Fabio' in *Wallpaper*, May-June, 49

Neumann, Nicolaus. 'Hot spot Milano' in *Elle Decoration* (D),
May-June, 182-183

Piccinelli, Roberto. 'After dark' in *Maxim*, July-August, 260

Piccinelli, Roberto. 'Bar Lodi' in *Trend*, June, 93

'Ein drink mit Andy Warhol' in *AD* (D), December-January, 18

'Full metal bar' in *D la Repubblica delle donne*, November, 86

'Fabio Novembre, el anàrquico exhibicionista' in *Diseño Interior*,
February, 25

'Neue bars' in *Hauser*, May, 16

1998

Finessi, Beppe. 'Pioggia di Novembre' in *Domus*, November, 96-103

Padovani, Maddalena. 'Abitare nomade' in *Interni Panorama*,
June, 60-63

Sironi, Fabio. 'Disco style' in *Carnet*, August, 100+

'Blu' in *Kult*, November, 122

1997

Casciani, Stefano. 'Il mondo salvato dai ragazzini' in *Abitare*, March, 177

Coz, Lauretta. 'Suggestioni psichedeliche' in *Casamica*,
September, 136-141

Coz, Lauretta. 'Vuoi copiare la mia?' in *Cento Cose*, May, 67-70

Morandi, Federica. 'Il fascino discreto dell'Atlantique' in *Locali*,
April, cover, 30-32

Pavarini, Maria Cristina. 'Acrylic obsession' in *Sportswear International*,
June, 64-65

Pavarini, Stefano. 'Acido blu, ufo, neon e ricci di mare' in *Lighting
Design*, May-July, 103+

Rolfini, Chiara. 'Blu, insegna anche a me la libertà delle rondini' in *Disco
& Dancing*, June, cover, 34-37

Semprini, Roberto. 'Nuova-mente' in *Interni*, June, 145-147

Wise, Bambina. 'Shopping under a psychedelic spell' in *South China
Morning Post*, January 26th, 6-7

'Dentro fuori' in *Ottagono*, June-August, 51

'Fabio Novembre, architecte et décorateur' in *Voyager*,
September, 92-93

'Fabio Novembre' in *W Fashion*, January, 46

1996

Boisi, Antonella. 'Come un fumetto' in *Interni*, October, 89+

Branzaglia, Carlo. 'Scambi reciproci' in *Stileindustria*, September, 42-44

Locati, Gioia. 'Usato e poi riciclato. Ma con tanta fantasia' in *Il Giornale*,
October 23rd, 41

Marchini, Simona. 'C'è un'opera d'arte nel bidone dei rifiuti' in *L'Unità*,
October 23rd, 22

Mazer, Lucia. 'E ora i rifiuti riciclati diventano opere d'arte' in *Il Giorno*,
October 23rd, 28

'Showtime' in *Architektur & Wohnen*, February, 22

'Loss of gravity in the M sector' in *MRD international*, March-April, 2+

'B2' in *Sing Tao Daily News*, December 4th, E3

1995

Comstock, Mireille. 'Worlds of angels, roses, and seduction' in *Yes*,
October, 63-65

Yeo, Ricki. 'All around the whirl' in *IQ*, June-July, 69-72

'Sex and shopping' in *Blueprint*, December-January, 12-13

'Fabio Novembre for Blumarine' in *Commercial Design*,
November, 142+

'Anna Molinari' in *Works*, November, 56-57

1994

Borgia, Marianna. 'Spazio di rappresentazione' in *Modo*, October, 34-35

Cawthorne, Zelda. 'Fit for the princesses' in South China Morning Post,
April 20th, 19

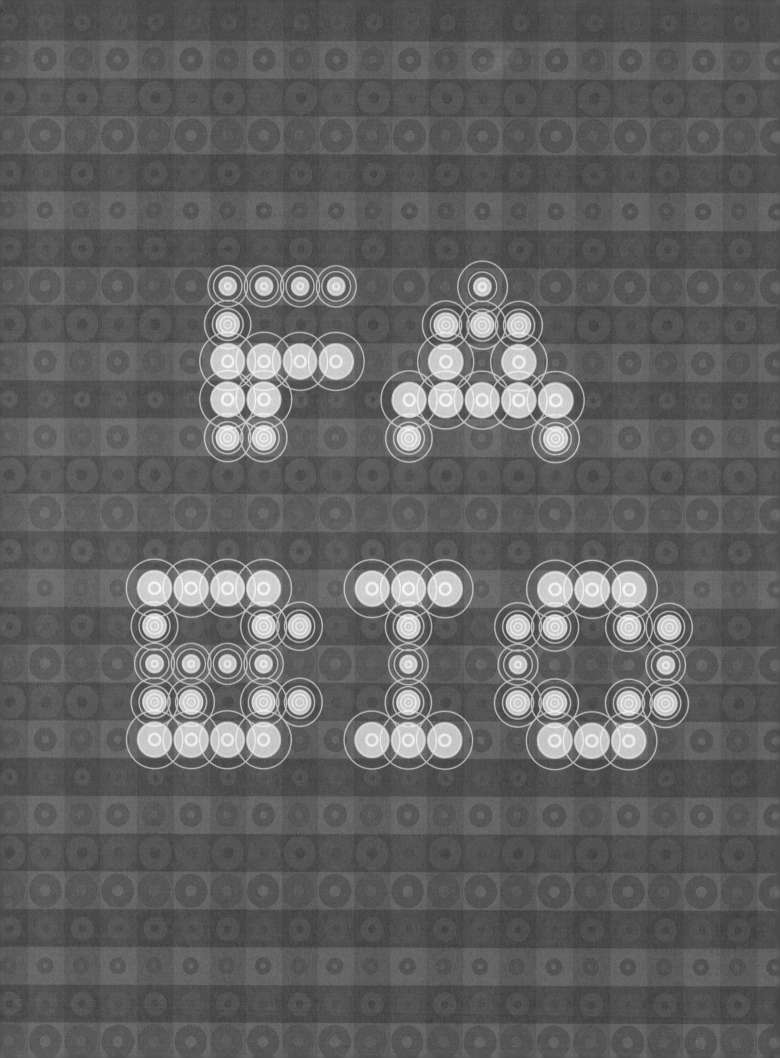